VICKY COULL

Troutbeck village ▶

CONTENTS

Text by Roly Smith

Also in this series:
The Peak District –
A Jarrold National Park
Guide

◀ *View over Mirehouse*
and Bassenthwaite Lake

Front cover pictures:
Rydal Water from White Moss
Common (main picture),
the House on the Bridge,
Ambleside (bottom left), the
steam yacht Gondola *on*
Coniston Water (bottom right)

THE LAKE DISTRICT

▼ *Ullswater from Hallin Fell*

THE LAKE DISTRICT'S unique mixture of lakes and mountains, dales and fells, makes it many people's favourite among Britain's National Parks.

The secret of the Lake District's appeal is in its scale, as William Wordsworth pointed out in his work *A Description of the Scenery of the Lakes* in 1822: 'I do not know of any tract of country in which, in so narrow a compass, may be found an equal variety in the influences of light and shadow upon the substance and beautiful features of the landscape.'

Although the highest ground around Scafell Pike, the tallest mountain in England, is only 3,210ft (978m) high, the rugged nature of the fells and the way they rise majestically from the lakes gives them the appearance of much loftier hills. However, the hilltops of the Lake District – sometimes cloud-covered but always green and inviting – are easily attainable by most fit walkers.

▲ *Hill Farm, near Langrigg*

◄ *Title page of Wordsworth's A Description of the Scenery of the Lakes, 1823*

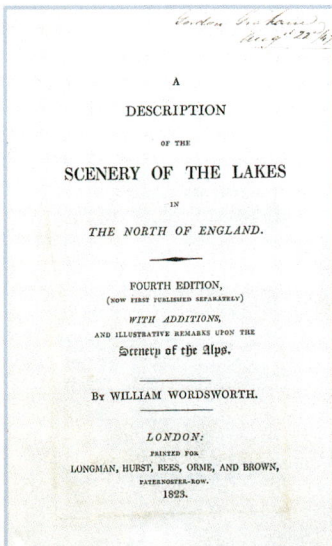

A

DESCRIPTION

OF THE

SCENERY OF THE LAKES

IN

THE NORTH OF ENGLAND.

FOURTH EDITION,
(NOW FIRST PUBLISHED SEPARATELY)

WITH ADDITIONS,
AND ILLUSTRATIVE REMARKS UPON THE
Scenery of the Alps.

BY WILLIAM WORDSWORTH.

LONDON:
PRINTED FOR
LONGMAN, HURST, REES, ORME, AND BROWN,
PATERNOSTER-ROW.
1823.

Many visitors are content to view the hills from the spectacularly beautiful valleys of the district, which radiate from a central point near Dunmail Raise on the A591 like the spokes of a water-filled wheel. Shaped initially by Ice Age glaciers and polished by aeons of wind and rain, the valleys are all different.

However, the physical features of the Lake District divide it naturally into three roughly parallel areas lying west to east. In the south is a band of gentle landscape stretching from Coniston Water, through the silvan beauties of Windermere to Kendal. The central zone runs from the stern, wild grandeur of Wasdale and Wast Water, where the craggy outlines of the highest hills watch over the deepest lake in England. In the north lie smooth, rounded hills, Derwent Water and the twin western lakes of

▲ *Steam yacht* Gondola
  on Coniston Water

Crummock Water and Buttermere.
The variety is astonishing, and
everybody seems to have their
favourite.

The major settlements of the
area are Kendal, the bustling little
town at the southern entrance to
the Lake District, and Keswick on
Derwent Water, 'capital' of the
less-visited and therefore quieter,
northern Lakes. The larger
villages include Ambleside,
Coniston, sheltering under its
Old Man, Grasmere, Hawkshead
and Bowness-on-Windermere,
which can become extremely
busy in the summer months.

▼ *Boats on Buttermere*

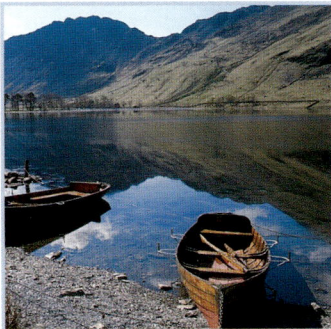

A brief history

Ever since prehistoric man
erected the enigmatic stone
circles at Castlerigg, near Keswick
in the north, and at Swinside, on
a shoulder of Black Combe in the
south-west, pastoral farming has
been the mainstay of the Lakeland economy. It still shapes the
landscape today.

The Romans interest in the area
was mostly military. They left their
roads and forts at Ravenglass,

▲ *The village of Ambleside
  in autumn colours*

▼ *Swinside stone circle*

▲ *Sizergh Castle with its Elizabethan extension, south of Kendal*

▲ *Wordsworth's famous daffodils beyond Gowbarrow Park*

Charcoal-burners, from the early 20th century ▶

region from the coast, leaving many common place-name endings such as '-thwaite' and words for physical features, such as 'beck', 'dale', 'fell', 'force', 'gill' and 'tarn'.

The area's medieval wealth was founded on the wool from the backs of the hardy Herdwick sheep, a breed superbly adapted to the harsh weather of the high fells. Monastic orders led the extension of sheep-farming by clearing woods and also exploited the minerals.

The stately homes of Sizergh Castle and Levens Hall, both near Kendal, were founded by gentry whose wealth was based on their extensive landholdings. The dry-stone walls of the Lake District are mostly a creation of the enclosure movement of the 18th and 19th centuries.

Both modern tourism and the idea of the national park can be said to have been initiated in the Lake District. The verse of the Lake Poets did much to popu-larise the area in the 19th century. Indeed, it was Wordsworth who, in his *Guide through the District of the Lakes*, published in 1835,

Hardknott and Ambleside, behind Hadrian's Wall to the north defending the northernmost frontier of the empire. After the decline of Roman power, the native Celts successfully resisted the Angles. The name 'Cumbria' has the same origin as the Welsh name for Wales, *Cymru*, and the Lake District's Celtic roots are still reflected in the local dialect. Norsemen later penetrated the

first suggested that the area should become 'a sort of national property, in which every man has an interest who has an eye to perceive and a heart to enjoy'.

Industry had touched the Lake District lightly, although there were significant green slate quarries at Honister and elsewhere, and productive copper mines at Coniston and lead (plumbago) mines in Borrowdale.

However, the growing commercial pressures on the Lake District from quarrying, reservoirs, forestry, and tourism by the arrival of the railways, gave birth to the beginnings of the conservationist movement. The Lake District Defence Society, later the Friends

Herdwicks – the traditional
▼ *breed of hardy Lakeland sheep*

of the Lake District, was founded in 1883. Canon Hardwicke Rawnsley of Crosthwaite, near Keswick, was one of the driving forces behind the foundation of the National Trust in 1895, whose earliest properties were acquired in the Lake District, and who now own around a quarter of the area.

◄ *Canon Rawnsley – founding spirit of the National Trust*

Canon Rawnsley's friend Beatrix Potter of Near Sawrey, left 14 farms and 4,000 acres (1,620 ha) of land to the Trust. However, formal National Park designation was not given until 1951.

The Lake District National Park is Britain's largest – covering 885 sq miles (2,292 sq km) – and it currently welcomes around 18 million visits a year. However, the Lake District retains its surprisingly unspoilt atmosphere, and visitors may still be reminded of what takes priority here when they are held up on one of the minor, drystone-wall enclosed roads that thread the dales and fells by a flock of sheep being taken for shearing.

KENDAL

THE 'AULD GREY TOWN' of Kendal, just outside the Lake District National Park, is one of several convenient centres for exploring the region.

The town is perhaps best known for Kendal mint cake, a confection that is much loved by hikers and climbers, and for the manufacture of 'K' Shoes. However, for six centuries after Flemish weavers were given permission to settle in the town in 1331, Kendal was known for manufacturing woollen cloth, especially the 'Kendal Green' favoured by archers, hence the town's motto *Pannus mihi panis* 'Wool is my bread'.

The local wool industry also gave rise to the small 'yards' or alleyways of Kendal, designed to allow easy road-to-river access. They are well worth exploring.

Near the Church of the Holy Trinity is Abbot Hall Art Gallery and Museum of Lakeland Life and Industry, where reconstructions present local life in previous centuries.

Kendal Castle – where the last wife of Henry VIII, Catherine Parr, was born – is now a ruin but offers a fine view over the town.

▼ *The River Kent, from which Kendal gets its name*

▲ *Dr Manning's Yard – one of many such courtyards in Kendal*

▼ *Kendal Castle*

TOWNEND FARM

The basis of farm and land control in the Lake District and border counties for many centuries was a form of customary tenure by 'statesmen'. These men owned the buildings, timber and everything on the land apart from the minerals under the soil as if it were their own, and such was their independence that until the Act of Union of 1603 they also had to contribute towards the defence of the Border.

An example of a typical Lake District statesman's house is Townend (*right*), near Troutbeck (just north of Bowness), which was in the hands of the Browne family for over four centuries and is now owned by the National Trust. It is a substantial building, dating back to the 17th century, with white, lime-rendered stonework, green slate roof,

WINDERMERE

The first 'surprise view' across
▼ *Windermere west from Kendal*

MANY PEOPLE'S INTRODUCTION to the Lake District comes as they head west along the A591 from Kendal and catch the first 'surprise view' down across Windermere, with the wooded Claife Heights beyond, from Banner Rigg.

Windermere – originally *Wynandremer* 'Vinandr's Lake' – takes its name from an early Norse settler and is England's largest lake. It stretches for 10½ miles (16.9km) from Newby Bridge almost to Ambleside, and always seems to be busy with pleasure craft of all descriptions.

The main settlement is the small town of **Windermere** (pop. 7,800), about a mile (1.6km) from the lake itself, which was founded when the railway reached the former hamlet of Birthwaite in 1847. **Bowness-on-Windermere** is the busy village on the lake shore, where steamers and other pleasure craft ply constantly across the island-studded waters. The Windermere Steamboat Museum, half a mile (800m) north of Bowness, has one of the world's finest collections of steamboats and organises trips on the lake.

There are National Park information centres at Bowness Bay and at Brockhole. The large Victorian mansion at Brockhole, between Windermere and

Windermere Steamboat
▼ *Museum at Bowness*

tall, cylindrical chimneys and oak-mullioned windows.

The interior of the farm, with its stone floors and dark, richly carved oak furniture, is preserved much as it might have looked three centuries ago. Added to over the years, Townend still retains its air of solid respectability, especially when viewed from its kitchen garden. Don't forget to see the weaving-gallery in the adjacent farm buildings.

▲ *Hawkshead Grammar School*

◀ *The gardens of the National Park Visitor Centre at Brockhole, Windermere*

Ambleside, was converted by the National Park Authority to a visitor centre in 1969. It has lovely lakeside views, interpretative displays, a bookshop and restaurant.

A cable-pulled ferry operates across the lake from Ferry Nab, just south of Bowness, to the western shore and the hamlet of **Near Sawrey**, the home of the children's author and illustrator Beatrix Potter, of Peter Rabbit fame (see panel below). Her former home of Hill Top is now a well-preserved museum, owned by the National Trust (NT) and dedicated to her life and works, which surprisingly included a fine reputation as a breeder of Herdwick sheep.

The car ferry across Lake Windermere ▶

The B5284 leads north along the quiet shores of **Esthwaite Water** to the white-painted buildings of the pretty village of **Hawkshead**. Thankfully now largely traffic-free, Hawkshead's cobbled courts and alleyways offer constant reminders of William Wordsworth, who was educated at the 16th-century grammar school, near the hilltop Church of St Michael's. There is

also the Beatrix Potter Gallery (NT), where other mementoes of her work are preserved.

A minor road from Hawkshead leads steeply uphill to the much-photographed beauty spot of **Tarn Hows** (NT), a lovely yet largely man-made landscape. The serpentine, tree-lined tarn was created by a dam that merged three smaller tarns into one, and the views from the higher paths of

BEATRIX POTTER

Generations of children have delighted in the tales of Peter Rabbit, Squirrel Nutkin and Jeremy Fisher – all characters from the prolific pen of Mrs William Heelis, wife of a solicitor

from Ambleside and better known as Beatrix Potter (*left*, at the age of 15).

All these gentle stories were inspired by the Lake District scenery Beatrix got to know first from family holidays and later as a resident at Hill Top farm (*right*) in the village of Near

Sawrey, which she bought from the royalties of her first book, *The Tale of Peter Rabbit*, published in 1900.

She settled in Near Sawrey after her marriage to William Heelis in 1913 at the age of 47, becoming a successful breeder of the local Herdwick sheep, and

▲ *The beauty spot of Tarn Hows*

▲ *The House on the Bridge, Ambleside*

Evening at Ambleside ▶

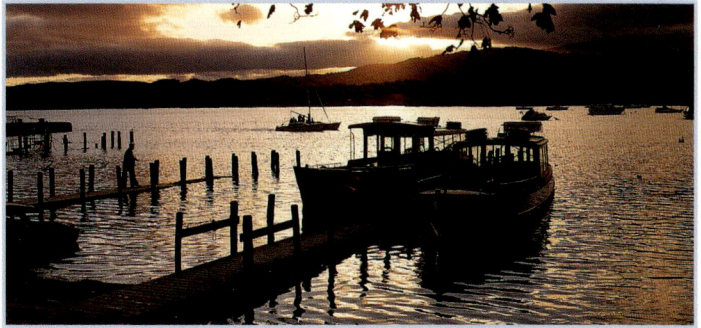

the higher fells such as rocky Wetherlam are justly famous.

Beyond Hawkshead, the B5286 leads around the head of Windermere to join the main road from Windermere village in Ambleside.

Ambleside (pop. 2,800), at the northern end of Windermere, is a mainly Victorian tourist centre for the southern and central Lakes, and cruises are run from Lakeside, a mile (1.6km) from its centre. Perhaps its most famous building is the House on the Bridge, which is a tiny, one-up, one-down building spanning the Stock Ghyll as it flows through the village and which now serves as a National Trust information centre.

using further royalties from her self-illustrated books to buy up farms around Hawkshead, Little Langdale and Coniston, Troutbeck and Buttermere to donate to the National Trust.

Many of the scenes from Beatrix Potter's charming books can readily be identified today, from the Tower Bank Arms at Sawrey (NT), which features in *The Tale of Jemima Puddleduck*, to the shores and islands of Derwent Water in *The Tale of Squirrel Nutkin*, and the slopes of Catbells in *The Tale of Mrs Tiggy-Winkle*.

The Tale of Tom Kitten and *Peter Rabbit* were obviously set at Hill Top, and today's visitors to the property – also owned by the National Trust – can still see those timeless settings in the carefully preserved interior.

CONISTON TO RAVENGLASS

THE BUSY VILLAGE of *Coniston*, at the northern end of Coniston Water, is dominated by the Old Man of Coniston, which rises to 2,635ft (803m). This is one of Lakeland's most popular peaks, rewarding climbers on fine days with views as far as the Isle of Man to the west and Blackpool Tower to the south. The usual approach is from the village by way of Church Beck and the Coppermines Valley. The name Coppermines Valley gives a clue to the real reason for Coniston's existence, for during the 18th and 19th centuries the hills to the west were the centre for an industry that thrived until cheaper imports flooded the markets. The ruined crushing mills, smelting plant and spoil heaps are especially obvious near the youth hostel in the Coppermines Valley, but these industrial remains are dangerous, so take care when exploring.

Coniston Water, at 5½ miles (9km) long, is a typically narrow, glaciated lake, and snakes southwards bordered by tree-shaded shores as far as Blawith. By far the best way of exploring the lake is in the Victorian splendour of the National Trust's superbly restored steam yacht *Gondola*, which plies a regular service from the pier at Waterhead during the summer months. This opulently fitted

Coniston Water from
▼ *Park-a-Moor*

BRANTWOOD

John Ruskin, poet, artist and critic, was one of the greatest figures of the Victorian age. He was also a social revolutionary who challenged the materialistic ethics of Victorian society and was one of the earliest conservationists.

Already in poor health, Ruskin came to live at Brantwood in 1872, bringing twelve gardeners with him, and having agreed to

▲ *Coniston village*   ▼ *Coniston Water*

yacht, described as 'a perfect combination of the Venetian Gondola and the English Steam Yacht' when built in 1859, was rescued in 1963 from life as a houseboat and lovingly restored to her former glory in 1980. The hour-long round-trip on the lake visits Park-a-Moor picnic site near the southern end of the lake, and makes a stop at John Ruskin's former home at Brantwood (see panel below), on the shore almost opposite Coniston village.

In 1937 the Forestry Commission bought an area of 8,000 acres (3,200ha) of the high ground between the lakes of Windermere and Coniston to develop as a forest. However,

buy the property without even having seen it but believing that any house with views of Coniston Old Man 'must be beautiful'.

Visitors can now judge the wisdom of Ruskin's sight unseen purchase;

Ruskin added that the views of the Old Man from the Turret are among the finest in the Lakes. The Brantwood Trust has restored the house to a condition much as Ruskin would have known it, and

there are regular exhibitions as well as displays of Ruskin's water-colour paintings and other works.

Ruskin's ideas have influenced such diverse intellectuals as Leo Tolstoy and Mahatma Gandhi, and

they live on in the environmental concerns that face today's world. He died at Brantwood in 1900 and is buried in Coniston churchyard.

unlike many of the Commission's sterile blocks of conifers, **Grizedale Forest** has always had public access as one of its objectives and has pioneered countryside interpretation and appreciation for visitors. Some fascinating and sometimes surprising modern sculptures, mainly in wood, adorn way-marked trails through the forest rides. There are also tree-top observation towers from which the forest's rich wildlife, which includes both roe and red deer, can be watched.

A deer museum was opened in 1956, and from this developed a fully fledged visitor centre, complete with audio-visual shows and craft demonstrations in the season.

▲ *Some of the many sculptures in Grizedale Forest*

▼ *Grizedale Forest Theatre*

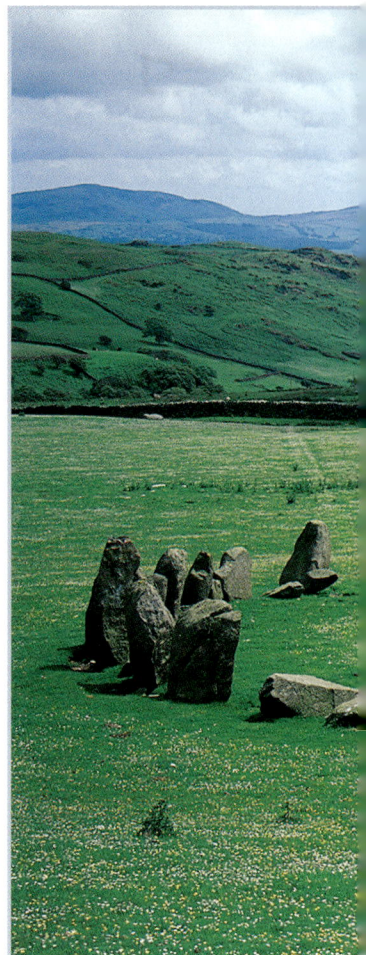

Grizedale's 230-seat **Theatre-in-the-Forest**, opened in 1970, enjoys an international reputation, staging over 100 performances each year. There is a highly acclaimed restaurant nearby.

The A595 leads south from Coniston around the great bulk of Black Combe, which shelters on

RAVENGLASS & ESKDALE RAILWAY

Modern tourists have every reason to be thankful that the Whitehaven Iron Mines company built a 3ft-gauge (0.91m) railway from Ravenglass to trans-port ore from the Nab Gill mines at Boot to the coast in 1875.

A year later the line was opened to passenger traffic, which continued after the mining company collapsed in 1882.

Later, the Ravenglass and Eskdale Railway was developed into a 15in-gauge (0.38m) passenger and freight line with a terminus at Dalegarth, just short of Boot.

Today the 7-mile (11km) line takes thousands of visitors into the heart of Upper Eskdale on regular excursions from the main-line terminus at Ravenglass, stopping at Irton Road, near Eskdale Green, and Dalegarth, near

▲ *The wide view from Swinside prehistoric stone circle*

its north-eastern flank the enigmatic stone circle of **Swinside**, reached by a minor road from Broadgate. This isolated neolithic monument occupies a sheltered moorland plateau on Swinside Fell, about 700ft (213m) above sea-level.

The road heads north towards **Ravenglass**, once the site of a Roman fort guarding the western coast. The remains of the fort's bath-house, known as Walls Castle, are still impressive. The village developed in the Middle Ages as an important market and port but declined after the Industrial Revolution and today is perhaps best known as the western terminus of the Ravenglass and Eskdale Railway.

The remains of the Roman
▼ *bath-house at Ravenglass*

Boot, and providing opportunities for walks 'between trains'. A museum at Ravenglass Station is devoted to the history of this fascinating line into the mountains, which has the affectionate local name of 'La'al Ratty'.

13

LANGDALE TO WASDALE

▼ *The Langdale Pikes*

THE HIGH POINT on the A591 Grasmere–Keswick road is known as Dunmail Raise, and the large cairn of stones that occupies the reservation between the carriageways is claimed to be the central point of the Lake District. It is also said to mark the burial cairn of King Dunmail, the last king of Cumberland, who was killed here in a Dark Age battle with the invading Scots. Certainly, you get the feeling that you are crossing a major divide as you breast the rise and the view extends down into the glacial trough now occupied by Thirlmere, with the heights of Helvellyn (3,118ft/949m) and Fairfield soaring away to the right. To the west, Steel Fell leads up across Grasmere Common to the triple summits of the **Langdale Pikes** and beyond them to Bow Fell and the Scafells – the highest ground in England.

Grasmere, nestling in the low ground between Great Rigg and High Raise, is perhaps best known for its association with William Wordsworth (see panel below) and he, his wife and sister Dorothy are buried in the churchyard of the Parish Church of St Oswald. Grasmere is also well known for its rush-bearing ceremony held in August, which recalls the days when all churches were carpeted with wild flowers and rushes, and the Grasmere Sports, held later in the month.

The **Langdale valley** is a mecca for walkers. It is reached by a minor road from Ambleside over Skelwith Bridge. Don't miss **Skelwith Force**, which is a short walk from the bridge.

The distinctive summits of the Langdale Pikes – Pike of Stickle,

The Grasmere rush-
▼ *bearing ceremony*

WORDSWORTH & THE LAKE POETS

It was William Wordsworth, born in Cockermouth on the edge of the Lake District in 1770 and educated at **Hawkshead Grammar School** between 1779 and 1787, who first popularised the Lake District through his poetry.

Works like *The Prelude* and *The Daffodils* made the area attractive to members of the *nouveau riche* of the Industrial Revolution and attracted many distinguished visitors and fellow writers and poets.

When William and his beloved sister Dorothy moved to **Dove Cottage** (*left*) at Grasmere in 1799, (now a Wordsworth museum, NT), Samuel Taylor Coleridge became a frequent visitor, having moved to Greta Hall,

▲ Looking across Grasmere

◄ Skelwith Force takes the combined waters of Great and Little Langdale

Harrison Stickle and Pavey Ark – are a common feature in many views of the central Lake District. Their ascent is a popular challenge to the fellwalker.

The last thing you would expect to find on the steep upper slopes of Pike of Stickle in the beautiful Great Langdale valley is a factory. However, that is exactly how a small site, discovered in

Keswick, with his brother-in-law, Robert Southey. Opium addict Thomas de Quincey was another of the Lakeland school, and later moved into Dove Cottage after William, now married to his childhood sweetheart Mary Hutchinson, had moved to **Rydal Mount** (*left*), on the road to Ambleside.

Much of Wordsworth's finest poetry was composed out-of-doors on long walks in and around the Grasmere area, often with the aid of copious notes written by Dorothy, who was a keen observer of the natural world around her.

◀ *The Wrynose Pass is still a testing route for travellers*

1947 just below the 2,362ft (709m) summit, has been described.

Here, neolithic people recognised that an outcrop of grey/green volcanic tuff produced stone that was hard enough to serve as axeheads. After being roughly shaped on site, these stones were transported to the coast near Ravenglass for final shaping and export all over

FARMING IN THE HILLS

The familiar close-cropped, treeless pastures of the Lakeland fells is not a natural landscape. It has been created by generations of shepherding in the hills.

Local breeds like the large, white-faced Herdwicks were specially bred to cope with the severe conditions that can be met on the fells. And don't be surprised if you see black lambs among the flocks – all Herdwicks

Britain. Langdale axes have been found as far away as the Yorkshire Wolds, Wessex and East Anglia.

The site, owned by the National Trust, is highly inaccessible and dangerous, and visitors should not try to reach it.

A minor road from **Elterwater**, at the foot of the valley, leads to Little Langdale and the famous motoring test of the **Wrynose and Hardknott passes**. This is a tortuous and difficult route, not for the inexperienced or faint-hearted. It winds up from Fell Foot across the Furness Fells between Swirl How and Ulpha Fell through Wrynose Bottom, and then, even more steeply, over the Hardknott Pass to drop down with magnificent views into Eskdale.

Just beyond the 1,291ft (394m) summit of the Hardknott Pass, to the right, lie the impressive remains of the **Hardknott Roman Fort**, which was known as Mediobogdum to the 500 unfortunate legionnaires who were stationed there around AD 120.

It used to be said that **Wasdale**, the deep scree-lined valley to the west of the Scafells, boasted the highest mountain, deepest lake, smallest church and biggest liar in England. The first three were, in order, Scafell Pike (3,210ft/978m); Wast Water (over 250ft/76m

▲ *The village of Elterwater and the Langdale Pikes from Skelwith Bridge*

The remains of the remote Roman fort that guarded ▼ *the Hardknott Pass*

are born black, and their fleece gradually turns grey with age.

The Herdwicks are an ancient breed, which was first developed on the monastic sheep ranches that covered the hills in the Middle Ages, but there are increasing numbers of black-faced, white-nosed Swaledales from Yorkshire these days.

The shepherd's life is a hard one, from lambing in the early spring through to dipping, shearing and gathering in the summer and autumn. He is aided by his faithful black-and-white collie dog, and this unique partnership between man and beast is put to the test annually at the many sheep-dog trials held at places like Patterdale and Kentmere.

In the valley bottoms, hardy black beef cattle are still kept, but they do not venture far up into the fells, which remain the domain of the hardy hill sheep and the equally hardy shepherd and his dog.

deep) and the tiny 39-seat Church of St Olaf at Wasdale Head. The final claim refers to Will Ritson, a 19th-century publican at the Wasdale Head Hotel, who boasted he told the world's tallest stories in annual competitions.

Wasdale certainly lives up to most of these superlatives, which are undoubtedly best appreciated on foot. Its rugged beauty has made it a popular place for serious hillwalkers and climbers. Indeed, the sport of rock-climbing is said to have been invented here by Walter Haskett Smith's first ascent of the Napes Needle on Great Gable at the head of the valley in 1886.

▲ *Fell Foot Country Park and Garden on Lake Windermere*

Thirlmere, a reservoir created in 1890–2, when two smaller
▼ *lakes were joined by flooding*

WILDLIFE IN THE HILLS

One of the most heartening stories of wildlife conservation in Britain in recent years has been the return of golden eagles to the Lake District. These majestic masters of the air were extinct in England for 200 years before they returned to Mardale, where they now breed successfully under the watchful eye of the Royal Society for the Protection of Birds (RSPB). It is hoped they may soon spread back to more of their old haunts in the high Lakeland fells.

Other more common birds to be seen on the felltops are the black,

PATTERDALE, ULLSWATER & HAWESWATER

Patterdale – said to have been visited by St Patrick in AD 540 ▶

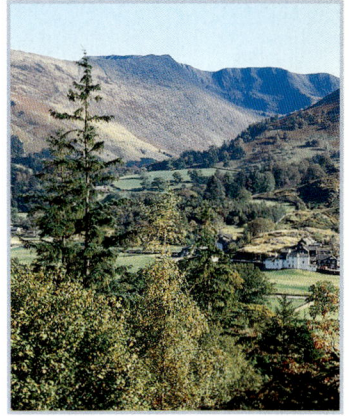

ULLSWATER IS MANY people's favourite lake because the scenery in its 8-mile (13km) length changes constantly, from the craggy, volcanic fells like Helvellyn, Raise and Gowbarrow at its southern end to the gentler slate landscapes around Pooley Bridge in the north.

The main A592 road from Windermere reaches Ullswater after crossing the impressive (1,489ft/454m) **Kirkstone Pass**, which takes its name from a large pointed rock said to resemble a church (kirk).

Ullswater views offer fells, meadows, woodland and ▼ *rocky shores*

Ullswater runs in three quite distinct reaches from **Patterdale**, a tiny farming hamlet at its head that takes its name from the Victorian Parish Church of St Patrick and is famous for its annual sheep-dog trials. There is always activity on Ullswater, from sailing-yachts and steamers operating from **Glenridding** pier to fishing along its shores.

The route to Helvellyn (3,118ft/ 949m) from the neighbouring hamlet of Glenridding via Striding Edge is one of the most popular and exciting in the district, but should only be attempted by experienced hillwalkers.

North from Glenridding, the A592 is a beautiful drive and

passes the turn to **Dockray** where a National Trust car park gives access to one of the Lake District's highest and loveliest waterfalls, **Aira Force**. Here the Aira Beck leaps 60ft (8m) down a precipitous tree-shaded gorge. A little further on, the road passes Gowbarrow Park on the left, which was the scene of William Wordsworth's famous poem in praise of daffodils. It used to be a deer park, and there are excellent walks with views over Ullswater.

Just over the fells of Martindale Common to the east lies the hidden valley of **Mardale**, reached from **Bampton**, near Shap. Mardale was flooded by the waters of the **Haweswater Reservoir** in 1937, but it still retains an air of unspoilt beauty, with high fells such as High Street and Harter Fell giving a real air of wilderness to the head of the reservoir, where there is a convenient car park.

croaking raven, the dashing peregrine falcon and the broad-winged buzzard, all of which have enjoyed a revival in recent years. The woodlands in the dale bottoms are the home of a good range of birds, including green- and red-spotted woodpeckers, nuthatch (*left*), tree-creeper and a variety of smaller songbirds. Crossbills can be seen in conifer plantations.

The largest mammals in the Lake District are deer, and there are sizeable herds of both red deer and roe-deer, which, if you are lucky, may occasionally to be seen on woodland edges.

One of the smallest mammals is the charming red squirrel, which in the Lake District is still the most common of Britain's two varieties of squirrel and was, of course, the inspiration for Beatrix Potter's character Squirrel Nutkin.

KESWICK TO COCKERMOUTH

DRIVING INTO THE Lake District from the M6 motorway on the A66, the great bulk of **Blencathra** dominates the skyline ahead and to the right. This 'Queen of the Northern Fells' carries the alternative name of Saddleback, and it describes perfectly the pronounced saddle between the summit (2,848ft/868m) and Foule Crag to the north, which is the top of Sharp Edge, a knife-edge of rock that provides one of the finest scrambles to any Lake District summit for the experienced fell-wanderer.

However, Blencathra is not the monarch of the Northern Fells. This distinction goes to neighbouring **Skiddaw** at a height of 3,053ft (931m), whose smooth and shapely slopes dominate the town of Keswick.

Skiddaw is an easy, though lengthy, mountain to climb, and the views from its stony summit of slate are superb, especially when looking south across Keswick and Derwent Water to the Central Fells.

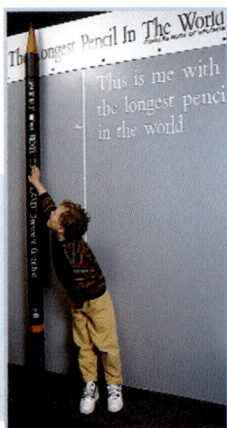

CUMBERLAND PENCILS

The longest pencil in the world (*left*) is among the many fascinating exhibits that are on display in the world-famous Cumberland Pencil Museum in the town of Keswick.

Pencils have been made at Keswick for over 150 years, and the reason for the industry being sited in this busy little market town is purely geological.

Deposits of the rare mineral plumbago, or black lead, were discovered in the Seathwaite valley in upper Borrowdale as early as the 16th century. It was originally used for glazing and hardening pottery,

◄ *Keswick's Moot Hall, dating from 1813, houses the local tourist information centre*

Derwent Water ►

▼ *Skiddaw seen over Derwent Water and Ashness Bridge*

Keswick is the 'capital' of the northern Lake District. It takes its name from the Old English for 'cheese farm', which indicates the type of pastoral farming that has been carried out in the low-lying plain between Derwent Water and Bassenthwaite Lake for generations.

Watched over by the clock tower of its white-quoined Moot Hall, which incorporates a tourist information centre, Keswick has a fine museum and art gallery and is now a busy tourist destination, especially in the summer season. The town is situated close to the shores of island-studded **Derwent Water**, one of the loveliest of the lakes, and regular boat trips ply its length from the landing-stage. A short walk from here is the famous beauty spot of **Friar's Crag** (NT), which takes its name from the monks who embarked from here to St Herbert's Island, where a hermit of that name lived in the 7th century.

Friar's Crag – a well-known beauty spot on Derwent Water ►

casting cannon-balls and as a preservative against rust.

By the early years of the 19th century, much of the plumbago, locally known as 'wad', was being used in the pencil factories at Keswick and Braithwaite.

Today, the Cumberland Pencil Company exports pencils of various colours and hardnesses all over the world using high-technology production methods.

◀ *The dramatic setting of Castlerigg stone circle*

under the western aspect of Skiddaw, is a little-frequented lake but one that is well known among birdwatchers for its visiting wild-fowl. **Bassenthwaite village** lies some distance from the lake itself, where a minor road leaves the A66 Keswick–Cockermouth route to cross the Whinlatter Pass over the Lorton Fells.

Cockermouth is a small market town on the north-western edge of the Lake District, best known for being the birthplace of William Wordsworth. The house (NT), dating from 1755, is now a museum to the poet's life, and several rooms have been furbished in the original style. Also worth visiting in Cockermouth is the Lakeland Sheep and Wool Centre, where about 20 different breeds of sheep are on view and sheep-dog demonstrations illustrate the Lake District's oldest industry.

Just outside Keswick on a minor road is the **Castlerigg stone circle** (NT), one of the most evocative of all the prehistoric monuments in the Lake District. This enigmatic neolithic circle, which Wordsworth described as 'a dismal cirque of Druid stones upon a forlorn moor', commands a spectacular view across to Blencathra and south to the Central Fells.

One of the most enduring trick questions on the Lake District concerns just how many lakes there are. The answer, of course, is one, because only **Bassenthwaite Lake** carries that appellation. Bassenthwaite Lake, north of Keswick and sheltering

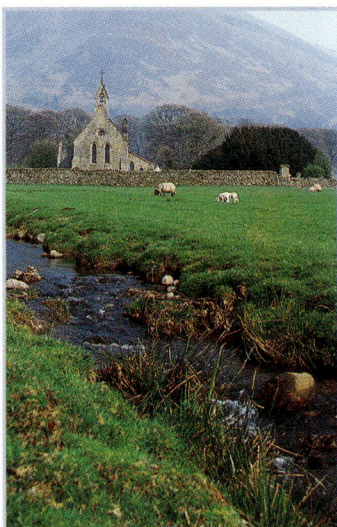

▲ *The Church of St Bega at Bassenthwaite*

Wordsworth House – the birthplace of the poet in Cockermouth ▶

D'YE KEN JOHN PEEL?

Fox-hunting and hound trailing have been traditional sports among the Lake District fells for centuries, and the most famous hunts-man was John Peel of Ruthwaite, near Caldbeck (*right*).

The Cumberland hunts bear little resemblance to the aristocratic sport of the shires further south. Here only the huntsman, or leader of the pack, wears red, and the dalesman, with his 'coat so grey' hunts on foot across the rugged fells, where horses are useless.

John Peel was born in Caldbeck in 1776 and was immortalised in the famous ballad written by his friend John Woodcock Graves, using an ancient border tune.

BORROWDALE TO BUTTERMERE

▼ *The Jaws of Borrowdale*

THE TOWN OF KESWICK is the best centre for exploring the 'hidden valleys' of Borrowdale and Buttermere, which take you into the rugged heart of the Lake District.

Borrowdale is approached on the B5289 through the narrow portals of the so-called 'Jaws of

The packhorse bridge in the
▼ *hamlet of Watendlath*

Borrowdale' at the southern end of Derwent Water. A side turn to the left at Barrow Bay leads onto a single-track road. This climbs past the much-photographed beauty spot of **Ashness Bridge**, with its fine views back across Derwent Water to Skiddaw, and eventually reaches the tiny Norse hamlet of **Watendlath**.

This is one of the Lake District's best-kept secrets – a lovely

▼ *The Bowder Stone*

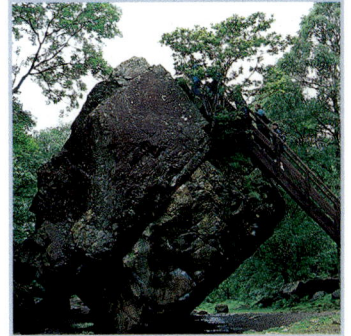

isolated settlement complete with charming packhorse bridge at the outlet of its own little tarn, and surrounded by high fells. It was the romantic setting for Hugh Walpole's novel *Judith Paris*. He also set his *Rogue Herries* in the Borrowdale area.

Back on the B5289, the road leads south between the shaggy slopes of the famous Borrowdale oak woods to pass the oddity of the **Bowder Stone**, a huge boulder 36ft (11m) high and weighing perhaps 2,000 tons that fell from the slopes of Grange Fell and can now be climbed by a wooden ladder.

A portrait of Peel hangs in the Oddfellows Arms in Caldbeck, where his elaborate gravestone, decorated with hunting symbols, is to be found in the churchyard (*left*). He died after a hunting accident near Ruthwaite in 1854.

▲ *Honister Pass*

Borrowdale widens out near the village of **Rosthwaite** before constricting again near the village of **Stonethwaite** and finally ending at **Seathwaite**, famous as being the wettest inhabited place in England with an annual rainfall of 120in (3,048mm). The suffix '-thwaite' is significant here and elsewhere in the Lake District because it comes from the Old Norse – the first settlers in the area – and indicates a clearing.

The B5289 leads right at **Seatoller** to cross the **Honister Pass** (1,190ft/362m) and descends steeply between the quarried crag of Honister on the left and Yew Crag on the right to the hamlet of **Gatesgarth** at the head of the lovely lake of **Buttermere**.

Once combined with larger **Crummock Water** to the north, Buttermere is hemmed in by dramatic fells, including Robinson, Red Pike, High Stile,

Buttermere is set in some of the most beautiful scenery in
▼ *the Lake District*

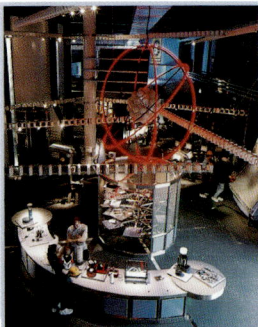

SELLAFIELD

Originally known as Calder Hall, then as Windscale and now as Sellafield, the world's first industrial nuclear power-station has become one of the county of Cumbria's top visitor attractions.

The ultra-modern Exhibition Centre at Sellafield (*left*) unfolds some of the mysteries of nuclear power and attempts to answer some of the controversies that surround it, including nuclear-fuel reprocessing, which is still carried on here. Using the latest computerised technology, exhibits and 'hands-on' demonstrations, 'the Sellafield experience' is aimed at all the family and provides a full day out. The visitor is guided through ten zones – including the interior of an atomic reactor and the globe-like

▲ *Crummock Water*

Hay Stacks and Fleetwith Pike. **Buttermere village**, with its famous Fish Hotel, lies between the two lakes on an alluvial fan, and there are pleasant, easy walks around the lake shores, including a recently reopened tunnel section, through magnificent scenery.

Ennerdale, a remote valley usually reached from Calder Bridge, is despoiled by the extensive forestry plantations at its head, but **Ennerdale Water** is one of the least spoilt or visited lakes. At the head of the valley, beyond the conifers and beneath the high fells of Pillar and Kirk Fell, stands England's most remote and primitive youth hostel at **Black Sail**.

◄ *The Fish Hotel in Buttermere village*

Ennerdale Water – little spoilt and little visited ▼

Earth House – all of which is available to wheelchair-users.

The first nuclear power plant at Windscale was built by the UK Atomic Energy Authority and opened in 1951, while the familiar twin cooling towers of the Calder Hall power-station followed five years later.

The plant is now run by BNFL (British Nuclear Fuels) and, in addition to being an important source of local tourism, is a significant employer of local people on the west coast of Cumbria.

THE LAKE DISTRICT NATIONAL PARK AUTHORITY

▼ *Brockhole Visitor Centre*

The purposes of the National Park Authority, which was reconstituted in 1997 to give greater representation to local people, are to:

- conserve the natural beauty, wildlife and cultural heritage
- promote opportunities for enjoyment and understanding
- foster the interests of the local community.

The Authority has to perform the difficult task of balancing the needs of the visitor to enjoy the landscape with its over-riding job of conserving it for future generations. If there is a conflict between conservation and

The Park Authority has a duty to foster the interests of the local community
▼

Wildlife conservation is
▼ *another duty of the Park*

recreation, the first duty is always paramount.

The 41,500 people who live within the 885 sq miles (2,292 sq km) of the Park are farmers, foresters, business people, a decreasing number of quarry or mineral workers, and an increasing number involved in tourism or associated service industries.

When the National Park was created in 1951, most people arrived by public transport and spent their holidays admiring the scenery from the valleys, with only a few hardy souls donning their boots and taking to the hills.

Today, the situation is quite different, with most visitors doing at least some walking, and 90 per cent of the estimated 18 million total of annual visitors arriving by car. At busy bank holiday weekends, the traffic jams to enter the Lake District can extend back to the M6 motorway, so the message is come early or, better still, outside the main visitor season.

To protect this precious landscape in the future, the National Park Authority may have to take some difficult decisions, and there could be some areas where the private car will be banned. Greater use of public transport will have to be encouraged and park-and-ride schemes introduced if the Lake District is not to be destroyed by its own popularity.

Lake District
National Park Authority

Murley Moss, Oxenholme Road, Kendal, Cumbria LA9 7RL
Tel 01539 724555

National Park visitor centre: Windermere, Brockhole
Tel 015394 46601
Open Apr–Oct daily
10.00–17.00

WHAT TO DO...

There are few areas in Britain which can offer such a variety of scenery and recreational opportunities as the Lake District. Whether visitors want to enjoy the unrivalled scenery from the valleys, take gentle strolls around the lakes or perhaps photograph or paint some of England's finest landscapes – or maybe test themselves against the elements and the landscape by the more active pursuits of hill-walking, rock-climbing, mountain-biking or yachting on the lakes – there are endless opportunities for all. But apart from its scenic beauty, the Lake District also has a large number of attractions, many of which may be suitable to visit on a rainy day.

Walking and outdoor activities

The majority of visitors come to the Lakes just to enjoy the land-scape, and the most popular way of doing that is by **walking** the fells. Many walkers have been inspired by the unique hand-scripted *Pictorial Guides* created by the late Alfred Wainwright, former borough treasurer of Kendal. Over nearly 40 years, Wainwright systematically explored all the Lakeland hills, tracing every route of ascent and most points of interest on the way in meticulous pen-and-ink drawings, maps and text.

Some of Wainwright's routes have become severely eroded by the passage of so many of his followers' boots, and path restoration has become a minor cottage industry in the Lake District as the National Park Authority and the National Trust attempt to repair the damage.

Access to the Lake District fells is usually unrestricted; a quarter of the area is owned by the National Trust. With 2,200 miles (3,540km) of public rights-of-way, including a network of ancient bridleways used by **pony-trekkers** and an ever-increasing number of **cyclists and mountain-bikers**, there is virtually free access for all. The new Cumbria Cycle Way is a 280-mile (450km) way-

Hiking through the
▼ *village of Troutbeck*

This is usually done in a sensitive way by the use of local stone and materials – and where diversions have been imposed while the work is being carried out, visitors should follow the official signs.

marked route around the edge of the county. The National Park runs **guided walks** every year (check locally for details), so that visitors can learn from experienced and knowledgeable leaders what there is to see.

SAFETY ON THE HILLS

Almost all the Lake District's summits are attainable by the fit and experienced walker, but the Lakeland hills are not to be underestimated, and no one should venture onto them without being properly equipped with boots, waterproof clothing and the knowledge of how to use a map and compass. Also, the weather on the fells is notoriously unpredictable, so always check the forecast before setting out (Weatherline, telephone 017687 75757). The moral is, if in doubt, turn back.

Most of the accidents on the fells are caused by walkers, although a few by climbers, making the Lake District mountain rescue teams among the busiest in the country. If you do get into difficulties, send for help and alert the rescuers by dialling 999.

▲ *Shap Abbey, south of Penrith*

The modern sport of rock-climbing was virtually invented in the Lake District, and it offers some of the most testing routes in Britain. But **rock-climbing** is for experts only, and there are a number of outdoor pursuit centres that can give instruction.

The lakes themselves, particularly Windermere, Coniston Water, Ullswater and Derwent Water, are highly popular with boating enthusiasts, although the National Park Authority has imposed speed limits on Ullswater and Windermere to prohibit the use of powerboats and water-skiers. It is claimed that these activities act against the aim of the National Park to provide opportunities for quiet open-air enjoyment. However, most **waterborne sports** are catered for, including sailing, canoeing, kayaking, windsurfing, rowing, self-drive hire, rafting and scuba diving.

The sports of **golf** and **fishing** are also well catered for in the Lake District. There are 15 golf courses in the area, some selling day tickets. If you plan to go fishing, apart from the rod licence a fishing-permit will be required.

Historic sites

Besides the more ancient historic monuments – such as the spectacularly sited **Castlerigg stone circle**, west of Keswick, or the **Roman forts** at Ambleside, Hardknott, and Ravenglass with its impressive bath-house – the Lake District has a variety of historic properties and other attractions open to the public.

Wordsworth's birthplace in Cockermouth, **Wordsworth House**, is extensively furnished in the original style. Also, his houses of **Dove Cottage**, with adjacent Wordsworth Museum, in Grasmere, and **Rydal Mount**, Ambleside, are open to visitors, as is **Hawkshead Grammar**

▲ *Hawkshead Grammar School*

School, founded in 1585, where Wordsworth received part of his education (see panel on page 14). While in the village, you may wish to visit 15th-century **Hawkshead Courthouse**, which has an exhibition on local life.

Brantwood, overlooking Coniston Water, where Ruskin spent his last days, is featured in the panel on page 10. A visit to Brantwood might profitably be combined with a round-trip on the National Trust's **steam yacht** *Gondola*, launched in 1859, which stops at Coniston Pier.

Most of the castles and abbeys of Cumbria are situated around the periphery of the Lake District. **Muncaster Castle**, near Ravenglass, has many attractions, not least its furniture, views, famous rhododendron collection and centre for the conservation of owls. **Sizergh Castle**, south of Kendal, is a mainly Elizabethan house with another fine garden and views, while Kendal and Penrith castles are romantic ruins.

North-east of Barrow-in-Furness lies **Furness Abbey**. Built of red sandstone in the 12th century, its impressive size reflects its former status as one of the richest abbeys in England. **Shap Abbey**, south of Penrith, was also founded in the 12th century, although most of the ruins date from the 13th. Nearby is the small, pre-Reformation Keld Chapel.

Perhaps the most charming of historic properties is Beatrix Potter's home, **Hill Top**, Near Sawrey. Originally a farmhouse, it is small and so visitor numbers are restricted. Another farmhouse to visit is **Townend**, at Troutbeck, a typical Lake District statesman's house dating from the 17th century (see panel on page 6).

Stately homes

Among the Lake District's stately homes is **Levens Hall**, south of Kendal, which is a fine Elizabethan mansion with a park and garden noted for its topiary, laid out from 1694; it also has a working steam collection. **Mirehouse**, by Bassenthwaite Lake, is more modest, built as a family home in 1666. Here the Spedding brothers entertained the leading literary figures of the 19th

▲ *Holker Hall, Cark-in-Cartmel*

century. **Holker Hall** at Cark-in-Cartmel near Grange-over-Sands, is known for its interior wood-carving and garden.

Museums, galleries and exhibitions

At the stately home of Holker Hall is the **Lakeland Motor Museum**, and nearby lies **Cartmel Priory Gatehouse**, dating from the late 12th century and now an art gallery and folk museum. There are many and varied museums and art galleries in the Lake District, ranging from the **Cars of the Stars Museum** in Keswick to the **Beatrix Potter Gallery** in Hawkshead. **Beatrix Potter's Lake District** in Keswick celebrates her

Chemist's Shop, Museum of
▼ *Lakeland Life and Industry*

life and work (see panel on page 8). Abbot Hall **Museum of Lakeland Life and Industry** in Kendal presents local life in previous centuries, some in the form of reconstructions.

Those with an interest in the industrial past may wish to visit **Stott Park Bobbin Mill**, Finsthwaite, Newby Bridge, which manufactured bobbins for the Victorian textile industry, or the **Cumberland Pencil Museum** in Keswick (see panel on page 20).

Sellafield Visitor Centre, on the coast at Seascale, presents nuclear power (panel on page 24), while enthusiasts for steam power will be drawn to the narrow-gauge **Ravenglass and Eskdale Railway** (panel on page 12). A rail trip on the standard-gauge **Lakeside and Haverthwaite Railway** may be combined with a cruise on Lake Windermere and a visit to the **Windermere Steamboat Museum**.

Brockhole, the Lake District National Park Visitor Centre at Windermere, offers exhibitions, audio-visual programmes and events as well as lake cruises and an adventure playground. The Forestry Commission has its visitor centre in **Grizedale Forest**, near Ambleside. There is also **Whinlatter Visitor Centre**, which has exhibitions at the start of the trails in Thornthwaite Forest, Braithwaite, west of Keswick.

Attractions for children

Many of the above attractions may interest children, like the Cars of the Stars Museum, Hill Top, or a trip on a steam railway or lake. Not only children will be drawn to the **World of Beatrix Potter Attraction**, Bowness-on-Windermere, which brings her stories alive with life-sized models of her characters and the new Mrs Heelis Film Theatre.

Holker Hall specially caters for children with their own guidebook.

▲ *On the Ravenglass and Eskdale Railway*

Another idea for a family day out is the National Trust's **Fell Foot Park and Garden** on the shore of Lake Windermere, where rowing-boats may be hired.

Sellafield Visitor Centre uses computerised technology and interactive displays to explain nuclear power.

Theatre

The performing arts have a distinctive venue in Grizedale's **Theatre-in-the-Forest**, which promotes high-quality events. The **Century Theatre** in Keswick also puts on significant productions.

FURTHER INFORMATION

Situated in the north-west corner of England, the Lake District is neatly bypassed by the M6 motorway and easily reached by train via the west coast London (Euston)–Glasgow line, from which a branch takes you to Oxenholme, near Kendal.

A good system of **public transport** allows you to leave the traffic jams behind and enjoy the scenery in comfort. Look out also for the white-painted Mountain Goat minibuses (Windermere 015394 45161 or Keswick 017687 73962) and the minibus transport offered by the National Trust. Cumbria County Council runs a Journey Planner Enquiry Line giving details of the buses, trains and ferries: 01228 606000 (Mon–Fri 09.00–17.00, Sat 09.00–12.00), http://www.ebguides.com/pubtrans/cumbria/info.html, or by post to Cumbria Journey Planner, Citadel Chambers, Carlisle CA3 8SG.

The following list of attractions gives details of opening times. However, these are liable to change. To be certain, ring the attractions direct, or contact the local tourist or National Park information centre. Details of these centres are also given below.

HISTORIC PROPERTIES

(EH = English Heritage; NT = National Trust)

Beatrix Potter's home, Hill Top (NT), Near Sawrey, near Ambleside.
Tel 015394 36269
Open Apr (Easter if earlier)–Oct Sat–Wed (also Good Fri) 11.00–17.00.

Brantwood, Coniston.
Tel 015394 41396
Open Mid-Mar–mid-Nov daily 11.00–17.30; Mid-Nov–mid-Mar Wed–Sun 11.00–16.00.

Dove Cottage and Wordsworth Museum, Grasmere.

Tel 015394 35544 or 35547
Open all year daily 09.30–17.30. Closed mid-Jan–early Feb and 24–26 Dec.

Furness Abbey (EH), Barrow-in-Furness.
Tel 01229 823420
Open Apr–mid-Oct Mon–Sat 10.00–18.00; mid-Oct–Mar 10.00–16.00

Hawkshead Courthouse, Hawkshead.

Tel 015394 35599
Open Apr–Oct daily 10.00–17.00

Hawkshead Old Grammar School
Tel 015394 36647 (evenings)
Open Easter–Oct Mon–Sat 10–12.30, 13.30–17.00, Sun 13.00–17.00. Closes 16.30 in Oct.

Holker Hall, Cark-in-Cartmel, Grange-over-Sands.
Tel 015395 58328
Open Apr–Oct Sun–Fri 10.00–18.00

Levens Hall, Kendal.
Tel 015395 60321
Open Apr–mid-Oct Sun–Thu: Grounds 10.00–17.00; House 12.00–17.00 (last entry 16.30); Steam Collection 14.00–17.00

Mirehouse, Bassenthwaite Lake.
Tel 017687 72287
House open Apr–Oct Wed and Sun 14.00–16.30 (last entry); Aug Wed, Fri and Sun 14.00–16.30 (last entry); Grounds and tearoom open daily 10.00–17.30

Muncaster Castle, Gardens and Owl Centre, Ravenglass.

Tel 01229 717614
Castle open Mid-Mar–end Oct Sun–Fri 12.30–16.00 (last entry); Gardens and Owl Centre open daily 11.00–17.00

Rydal Mount and Gardens, Ambleside.
Tel 015394 33002
Open Mar–Oct daily 09.30–17.00; Nov–Feb Wed–Mon 10.00–16.00.

Sizergh Castle (NT), Sizergh, near Kendal.
Tel 015395 60070
Open Apr–Oct Sun–Thu 13.30–17.30

Stott Park Bobbin Mill (EH), Finsthwaite, Newby Bridge.

Tel 01539 531087
Open Apr–Oct daily 10.00–18.00 or dusk if earlier

Townend Farm (NT), Troutbeck, Windermere.
Tel 015394 32628
Open Apr–Oct Tue–Fri, Sun and bank hol. Mon 13.00–17.00 or dusk if earlier

Wordsworth House (NT),
　Main Street, Cockermouth.

Tel 01900 824805
Open Apr–Oct Mon–Fri
(Sat in July and Aug) 11.00–17.00.
Phone for other Sat.

MUSEUMS, GALLERIES & EXHIBITIONS

Abbot Hall Art Galley and Museum of Lakeland Life and Industry,
　Kirkland, Kendal.
　Tel 01539 722464
　Open all year daily 10.30–17.00.
　Reduced hours from 1 Nov.

Beatrix Potter Gallery (NT), Main
　Street, Hawkshead.
　Tel 015394 36355
　Open Apr–Oct Sun–Thu
　10.30–16.30 (last entry 16.00).

Beatrix Potter's Lake District (NT),
　Packhorse Court, Keswick.
　Tel 017687 75173
　Open Apr–June, Sept and Oct daily
　10.00–17.00; July and Aug daily
　10.00–17.30; Nov–Mar
　Sat and Sun 12.00–16.00

Cars of the Stars Motor Museum,
　Standish Street, Keswick.
　Tel 017687 73757
　Open mid-Feb–early Jan daily
　10.00–17.00

Cartmel Priory Gatehouse (NT) **and
　church**, Cavendish Street, Cartmel.

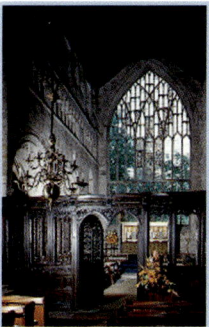

Tel 015394 35599
Open Apr–Oct Tue–Sun 11.00–17.00.

Cumberland Pencil Museum,
　Southey Works, Keswick.
　Tel 017687 73626
　Open all year daily 09.30–16.00
　(last entry). Closed Christmas and
　New Year

**Dove Cottage and Wordsworth
　Museum**, Grasmere.
　Tel 015394 35544 or 35547
　Open all year daily 09.30–17.30.
　Closed Jan, early Feb and
　24–26 Dec.

Heaton Cooper Studio, Grasmere.
　Tel 015394 35280
　Open summer Mon–Sat
　09.00–18.00, Sun 12.00–18.00;
　winter Mon–Sat 09.00–17.00,
　Sun 12.00–17.00

Kendal Museum,
　Station Road, Kendal.
　Tel 01539 721374
　Open Apr–Oct 10.30–17.00;
　1–24 Nov 10.30–16.00

**Keswick Park Museum
　and Art Gallery,**
　Station Road, Keswick.
　Tel 017687 73263
　Open Easter–Oct daily 10.00–16.00

Lakeland Motor Museum,
　Holker Hall, Cark-in-Cartmel.
　Tel 015395 58509
　Open Apr–Oct Sun–Fri 10.30–17.00

Lakeland Sheep and Wool Centre,
　Egremont Road, Cockermouth.

Tel 01900 822673
Open daily 09.00–16.00

Windermere Steamboat Museum,
　Rayrigg Road, Windermere.
　Tel 015394 45565
　Open Easter–Oct
　daily 10.00–17.00

World of Beatrix Potter Attraction,
　Crag Brow,
　Bowness-on-Windermere.
　Tel 015394 88444
　Open Oct–Easter daily 10.00–16.00;
　Easter–Sept daily 10.00–16.30

OTHER ATTRACTIONS

**Brockhole Lake District National
　Park Visitor Centre**,
　Windermere.

Tel 015394 46601
Open Apr–Oct daily 10.00–17.00

Fell Foot Park and Garden (NT),
　Newby Bridge.
　Tel 015395 31273
　Open all year daily 10.00–dusk

Grizedale Forest Visitor Centre
　(Forest Enterprise),
　Grizedale, Ambleside.
　Tel 01229 86001
　Open Feb–Mar, Nov–Jan
　Mon–Fri 10.00–16.00,
　Sat and Sun 10.00–17.00;
　Apr–Oct daily 10.00–17.00
　(July –17.30)

Lakeside and Haverthwaite Railway,
　Lakeside.
　Tel 015395 31594
　Open Easter week, then weekends
　until early May, then daily until the
　end of Oct.

Ravenglass and Eskdale Railway
　Tel 01229 717171
　Open late Mar–early Jan daily.
　Closed 23–25 Dec.

Sellafield Visitor Centre,
　Sellafield, Seascale.
　Tel 019467 27027
　Open Apr–Oct daily 10.00–18.00;
　Nov–Mar daily 10.00–16.00.
　Closed Christmas Day

Steam yacht *Gondola* (NT),
　Brantwood/Coniston.
　Tel 015394 41288
　Open Apr (Easter if earlier)–Oct daily
　sailings from 11.00 (Sat 12.05)

Whinlatter Forest Visitor Centre,
　Braithwaite, Keswick.
　Tel 017687 78469
　Open Feb–Dec daily 10.00–17.30

THEATRES

Century Theatre,
　Lakeside, Keswick.
　Tel 017687 74411

Theatre-in-the-Forest, Grizedale.
　Tel 01229 860291

LAKE DISTRICT NATIONAL PARK AUTHORITY

Murley Moss, Oxenholme Road,
Kendal, Cumbria LA9 7RL.
Tel 01539 724555

National Park visitor centre:
Windermere, Brockhole.
Tel 015394 46601
Open Apr–Oct daily 10.00–17.00

National Park information centres

(*not open all year):

*Ambleside:** Waterhead.
Tel 015394 32729

*Bowness Bay:** Glebe Road,
Bowness-on-Windermere.
Tel 015394 42895

*Coniston:** Main Car Park,
Ruskin Avenue.
Tel 015394 41533

*Grasmere:** Red Bank Road.
Tel 015394 35245

*Hawkshead:** Main Car Park.
Tel 015394 36525

Keswick: Moot Hall.
Tel 017687 72803

*Pooley Bridge:** The Square.
Tel 017684 86530

*Seatoller:** Seatoller Barn, Borrowdale.
Tel 017687 77294

*Ullswater:** Main Car Park,
Glenridding.
Tel 017684 82414

CUMBRIA TOURIST BOARD

Ashleigh, Holly Road,
Windermere, Cumbria
LA23 2AQ.
Tel 015394 44444;
Fax 015394 44041;
Internet: http://www.cumbria.gov.uk;
Web site: http://www.cumbria-the-lake-district.co.uk

Tourist information centres

(*not open all year):

Ambleside: Market Cross.
Tel 015394 32582

Barrow-in-Furness: Duke Street.
Tel 01229 870156

*Bowness-on-Windermere:**
Glebe Road.
Tel 015394 42895

*Broughton-in-Furness:**
Town Hall, The Square.
Tel 01229 716115

Cockermouth: The Town Hall.
Tel 01900 822634

*Coniston:** Main Car Park,
Ruskin Avenue.
Tel 015394 41533

Egremont: 12 Main Street.
Tel 01946 820693

Grange-over-Sands:
Victoria Hall, Main Street.
Tel 015395 34026

*Grasmere:** Red Bank Road.
Tel 015394 35245

*Hawkshead:** Main Car Park.
Tel 015394 36525

Kendal: Town Hall, Highgate.
Tel 01539 725758

Keswick: Moot Hall,
Market Square.
Tel 017687 72645

*Killington Lake:** M6 (southbound),
near Kendal.
Tel 015396 20138

Maryport: Senhouse Street.
Tel 01900 813738

Penrith: Robinson's School,
Middlegate.
Tel 01768 867466

*Pooley Bridge:** The Square.
Tel 017684 86530

*Seatoller:** Seatoller Barn.
Tel 017687 77294

Sellafield: Visitor Centre.
Tel 019467 76510

Southwaite: M6 Service Area.
Tel 016974 73445/6

*Ullswater:** Main Car Park,
Glenridding.
Tel 017684 82414

Ulverston: Coronation Hall,
County Square.
Tel 01229 587120

*Waterhead:** Car Park.
Tel 015394 32729

Whitehaven: West Strand.
Tel 01946 852939

Windermere: Victoria Street.
Tel 015394 46499

FRIENDS OF THE LAKE DISTRICT

3 Yard 77, Highgate,
Kendal, Cumbria LA9 4ED.
Tel 01539 720788

NATIONAL TRUST

Tel 015395 31273 or
015394 35599

National Trust information centres:

Ambleside: Bridge House
Keswick: Lakeside
Hawkshead: The Square
Cockermouth: Wordsworth House
Newby Bridge: Fell Foot Country Park

LAKE DISTRICT WEATHERLINE

Tel 017687 75757

The following pictures are reproduced by courtesy of
BNFL: page 18; Cumbria Tourist Board: page 13 (bottom right); John Curtis: outside front cover (main picture); Lake District National Park Authority: page 26 (logo); Muncaster Castle: page 30 (top right); National Trust Photographic Library: page 8 (bottom left); Ravenglass & Eskdale Railway Ltd: page 13 (bottom left); Museum of Lakeland Life & Industry, Kendal: page 4 (bottom); Wordsworth Trust, Dove Cottage, Grasmere: pages 2 (bottom) & 5 (top).

ISBN 0-7117-1010-4 © Jarrold Publishing 1999.
Published by Jarrold Publishing, Norwich. Printed in Great Britain. 1/99